■SCHOLASTIC

PHONICS
PUZZLES & GAMES

50+ Skill-Building Activities
for Reading Success

CINDI MITCHELL

Editor: Maria L. Chang
Cover design: Cynthia Ng
Interior design: Grafica Inc.
Puzzle Illustrations © Jim and Cindi Mitchell
Art spots: Rob McClurkan, The Noun Project, Doug Jones
All other images © Shutterstock.com.

ISBN: 978-1-5461-1381-2
Scholastic Inc., 557 Broadway, New York, NY 10012
Copyright © 2024 by Cindi Mitchell
Published by Scholastic Inc. All rights reserved.
Printed in the U.S.A.
First printing, January 2024.
1 2 3 4 5 6 7 8 9 10   40   33 32 31 30 29 28 27 26 25 24

Contents

Introduction

Welcome to *Phonics Puzzles & Games*!
We are excited to share this collection of 50+ fun and engaging phonics activities with you. Research shows that phonics instruction is an essential ingredient in learning how to read. According to phonics expert Jeanne Chall, "By learning phonics, students make faster progress in acquiring literacy skills—reading and writing. By the age of 6, most children already have about 6,000 words in their listening and speaking vocabularies. With phonics they learn to read and write these and more words at a faster rate than they would without phonics." This book is chock-full of activities that provide children with opportunities to gain decoding skills so they can recognize words quickly and accurately. Children practice identifying consonants, short and long vowels, complex vowels, consonant blends, digraphs, and more. As they learn various strategies for figuring out unfamiliar words, their automatic word recognition will improve, which in turn will boost their fluency, comprehension, and desire to read.

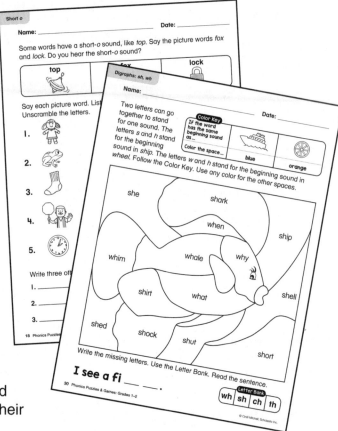

While we created these activities to reinforce specific phonics skills, we intentionally designed them to stimulate children's imaginations and to tap into their natural desire to learn, play, and have fun. Within these pages you will find crossword puzzles, mystery pictures, word searches, word ladders, writing activities, and more. We hope your students find these activities enjoyable and challenging as they build a solid foundation in phonics and embark on a path toward reading and writing success!

How to Use This Book

Use the activities in this book to supplement your reading program. They are ideal for practice, review, or homework. Each puzzle, activity, and game reinforces a specific literacy skill. The only materials children will need for most activities are a pencil, crayons, or colored pencils. For the games, you will find the items you need clearly written at the beginning of each game. Here are the types of activities you will find inside:

- **Crossword Puzzle:** Using a Word Bank and picture clues, children fill in a crossword puzzle based on the featured phonics skill.

- **Dot-to-Dot:** Children use their phonics knowledge to answer questions. They then use their answers to connect dots and reveal a mystery picture, which they can color.

- **Maze:** In a field of shapes, children find their way through a maze by identifying words that contain the featured phonics element and then coloring in those shapes.

- **Picture Puzzle:** Using a Color Key, children color parts of a mystery picture based on the phonics elements of the words in the spaces. After they have colored in each space, children use a Letter Bank to complete a sentence below the puzzle.

- **Unscramble:** Using pictures and definitions as clues, children unscramble letters to create words.

- **Word Ladder:** Children start at the bottom of the puzzle and work their way to the top by changing one letter of a word on each rung of the ladder.

- **Word Search:** Children hone their letter sound-recognition skills as they complete word searches.

- **Word Sort:** Children sort words based on various characteristics.

- **Writing Activity:** Children solve themed riddles and then write a response to prompts.

- **Games:** What better way to teach phonics than through games? Engage children with these playful games that promote phonics and word-study skills. The games include relay races, guessing games, card games, and scavenger hunts.

Extend Student Learning

Phonics instruction at its best doesn't stop when formal instruction is done. Take opportunities to pause throughout the day and engage in some quick phonics and word-study activities. Here are a few suggestions:

- **Take a five-minute break and use a beach ball to play Alphabet Catch.** The first player says a word that begins with an /a/ sound, such as *apple*. Then the player tosses the ball to another player. The receiving player says a word that begins with a /b/ sound, such as *bell*, and so on. Play continues as players toss the ball and work their way through the alphabet.

- **Pair up children.** Write a long-*a* phonogram on the board, such as *-ake*. Challenge children to work with their partner and add one or two letters to the beginning of the phonogram to make as many new words as possible; for example, *rake*, *bake*, and *shake*. Have each pair share their words with the class. Then, introduce a different phonogram and start again.

- **Play this silly game to practice alliteration while having fun.** Start the game by saying: *Silly Sam is going to the seashore. He can only take items that begin with an /s/ sound.* One at a time, invite children to name something that Sam might take with him, such as *sandwiches*, *swimsuits*, *sandals*, *salsa*, and a *sailboat*. When children can't think of any more words, create a new scenario, and start again with a different letter sound.

- **This is a great activity to use in the classroom after studying prefixes.** Tell children that we often use prefixes in our speech and don't even stop to think about it. As a class, come up with a list of common words that have prefixes and write them on the board. Put children on a "Prefix Alert" for the day. Any time they read or hear a word with a prefix, have them add it to the list of prefixes on the board. Repeat the activity, but this time have children look for words that have suffixes instead of prefixes.

- **Share some two-line rhymes with children.** Point out that each rhyme has two lines and the last word in each line rhymes.

Tommy rides his bike fast. *He doesn't want to be last.*	*High-jumping dolphins were fun to see* *Until they splashed water all over me.*

Write pairs of rhyming words on the board: *rat, hat; hen, pen; bake, cake; fish, wish; rest, best.* Challenge children to use one of the rhyming pairs to write their own two-line rhyme.

Meeting Core Language Arts Standards

The activities in this book meet the following foundational skills standards for Grades 1–2.

PHONOLOGICAL AWARENESS	
RF.1.2	Demonstrate understanding of spoken words, syllables, and sounds (phonemes).
RF.1.2.A	Distinguish long from short vowel sounds in spoken single-syllable words.
RF.1.2.B	Orally produce single-syllable words by blending sounds (phonemes), including consonant blends.
RF.1.2.C	Isolate and pronounce initial, medial vowel, and final sounds (phonemes) in spoken single-syllable words.
RF.1.2.D	Segment spoken single-syllable words into their complete sequence of individual sounds (phonemes).
PHONICS AND WORD RECOGNITION	
RF.1.3, RF.2.3	Know and apply grade-level phonics and word analysis skills in decoding words.
RF.1.3.A	Know the spelling-sound correspondences for common consonant digraphs.
RF.1.3.B	Decode regularly spelled one-syllable words.
RF.1.3.C	Know final-*e* and common vowel team conventions for representing long-vowel sounds.
RF.1.3.D	Use knowledge that every syllable must have a vowel sound to determine the number of syllables in a printed word.
RF.2.3.A	Distinguish long and short vowels when reading regularly spelled one-syllable words.
RF.2.3.B	Know spelling-sound correspondences for additional common vowel teams.
RF.2.3.D	Decode words with common prefixes and suffixes.

Name: _____   **Date:** _____

Say each picture word below. Listen for the *beginning* sound.
Then, follow the Color Key.

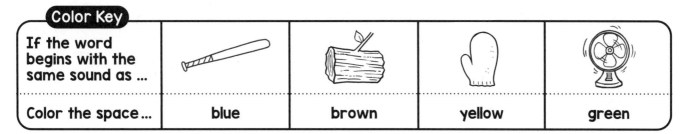

Color Key				
If the word begins with the same sound as ...	🏏	🪵	🧤	🌀
Color the space ...	**blue**	**brown**	**yellow**	**green**

Use any color for the other spaces.

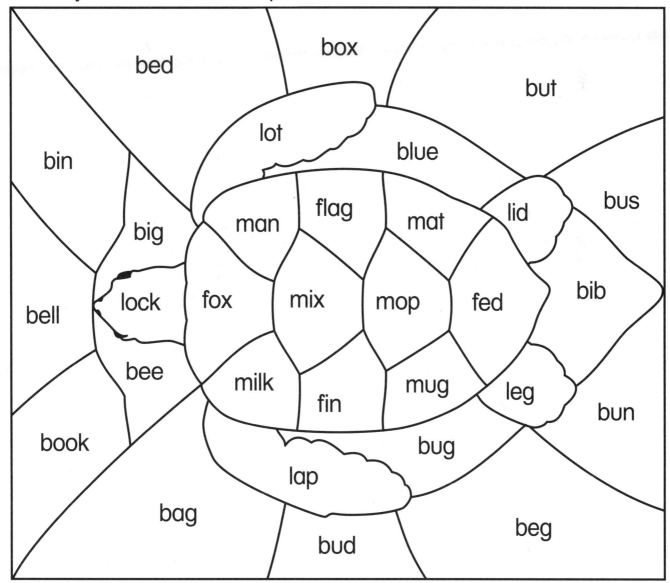

Write the missing letter. Use the Letter Bank. Read the sentence.

I see a big ___urtle.

Letter Bank			
b	l	m	t

Name: _____   **Date:** _____

Say each picture word below. Listen for the *ending* sound.
What letter stands for the ending sound? Circle it.
Then, connect the dots in the order of the answers. Start at the ♥.

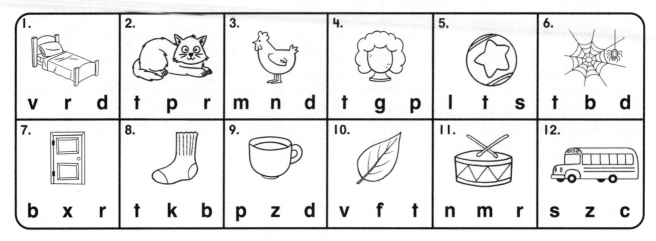

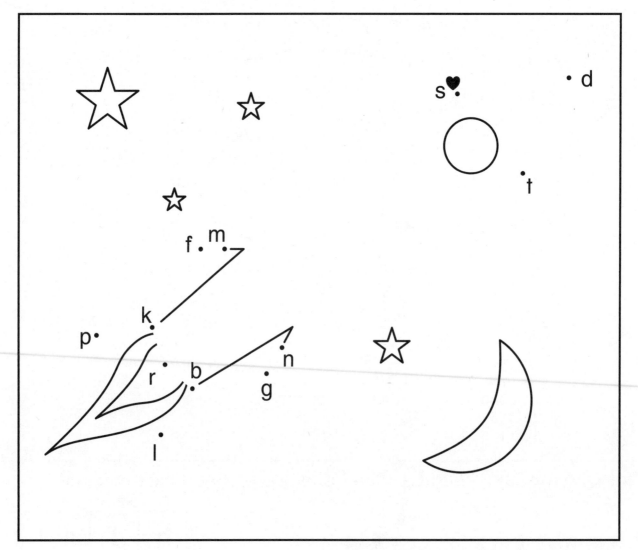

Name: _____   **Date:** _____

The letter *d* stands for the beginning sound you hear in *dance*.
The letter *m* stands for the ending sound you hear in *jam*.
Help the bunnies get to the garden. Follow the Color Key.

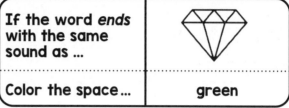

Color Key			
If the word *begins* with the same sound as ...	🐕	If the word *ends* with the same sound as ...	💎
Color the space...	orange	Color the space...	green

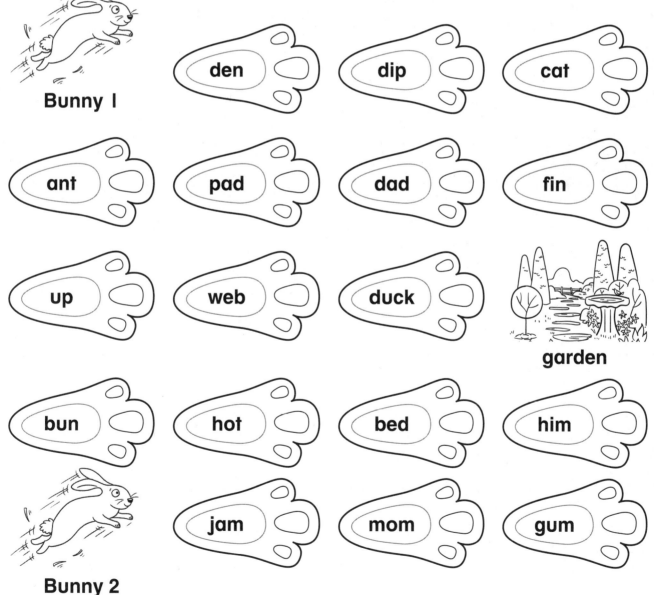

Bunny 1

den   dip   cat

ant   pad   dad   fin

up   web   duck   garden

bun   hot   bed   him

Bunny 2   jam   mom   gum

Name: _____   Date: _____

Some words have letters that are silent.
Say the picture words *wreck* and *climb*.
Wreck has a silent letter *w*.
Climb has a silent letter *b*.

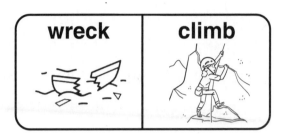

| wreck | climb |

Say each picture word. Unscramble the letters. Circle the silent letter.

1. 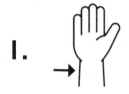   s t i w r   __ __ __ s __

2. 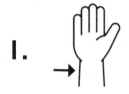   a b l m   __ a __ __

3.    o c b m   __ __ m __

4.    t i e w r   __ __ __ __ e

5.    h t b m u   __ __ __ m __

Write the picture words below.

Words with a silent *w*	Words with a silent *b*
_____	_____
_____	_____
	_____

Name: _____   **Date:** _____

Finish the Story

Look at the pictures. Write the missing letters.
Use the Letter Bank. Then, read the story.

Letter Bank					
r	b	c	h	p	d

Ready to Play!

Sam is a ___og.

He loves to play in the ___ain.

Sam puts on one rain ___at.

Sam puts on one rain ___oat.

Sam puts on one pair of rain ___ants.

How many rain ___oots does Sam put on?
Four, of course!

Write About It

What does Sam do next?

_____

_____

Name: _____ **Date:** _____

The letter *c* can stand for two sounds. It stands for the soft-*c* sound in *circle*. It stands for the hard-*c* sound in *cat*.

Say each picture word. If the word has a soft-*c* sound, circle it blue. If it has a hard-*c* sound, circle it red.

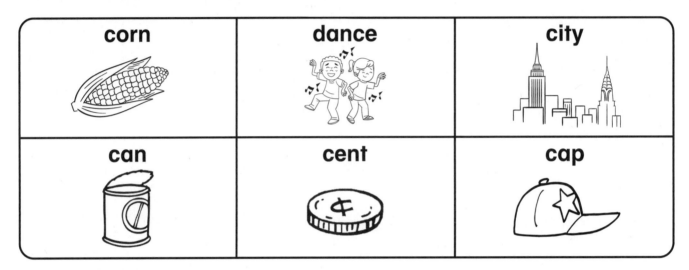

corn	dance	city
can	cent	cap

Find the picture words below. Circle them.
The words may go across or up and down.

b   d   v   c   a   n

c   a   p   o   l   c

j   n   w   r   c   i

v   c   r   n   e   t

c   e   n   t   r   y

Name: _____ **Date:** _____

The letter *g* can stand for two sounds. It can stand for the hard-*g* sound in *gate*. It can also stand for the soft-*g* sound in *giant*.

Say each picture word. If the word has a soft-*g* sound, write it under **Soft *g***. If it has a hard-*g* sound, write it under **Hard *g***.

leg 	gem 	gift 	cage 
gate 	log 	guitar 	giraffe 

Soft *g*	Hard *g*

Name: _____ **Date:** _____

Animal Riddles

Word Bank

| giraffe | pigeon | goose | goat |

Read each clue. Write the answer. Use the Word Bank.

1. I rhyme with *boat*.
But I don't have one.   _____

2. I rhyme with *moose*.
But I don't have four legs.   _____

3. I can fly hundreds of miles a day.
But I am not an airplane.   _____

4. I have a long neck.
But I am not a swan.   _____

Write About It

Choose one animal above. Don't tell anyone. Write clues about the
animal. Have a friend read the clues and guess the secret animal.

Clues

1. _____

2. _____

3. _____

Name: _____   **Date:** _____

Some vowels have a short-*a* sound, like *bat*. Say each word in the Word Bank. Listen for the short-*a* sound. Underline the letter that stands for the short-*a* sound.

Word Bank

cat	cap	bag	hand
mat	mask	flag	fan

Write the picture word below. Use the Word Bank to help. Then fill in the puzzle.

Across

2. _____

4. _____

5. _____

7. _____

Down

1. _____

2. _____

3. _____

6. _____

Name: _____ **Date:** _____

Some vowels have a short-*e* sound, like *bed*.

Start at the bottom of the ladder. Say the word *ten*. Do you hear the short-*e* sound? Climb up the ladder and say the next picture word. Use the clues. Write the word.

6. ___ ___ ___

Change one letter.

5. ___ ___ ___

Change one letter.

4. ___ ___ ___

Change one letter.

3. ___ ___ ___

Change one letter.

2. ___ ___ ___

Change one letter.

1. **10**   t   e   n

Name: _____   Date: _____

Some words have a short-*i* sound, like *pin*. Say the picture words *wig* and *six*. Do you hear the short-*i* sound?

| pin | wig | six |

Help the chick find its mother. Read the words below. If a word has a short-*i* sound, color the shape blue. Then, follow the blue shapes.

big	bat	ten	cot
dip	in	man	sat	dog
lip	pet	hop	mat	cup
win	fin	sit	gem	sum
dam	net	pit	fix	

Name: _____ Date: _____

Some words have a short-*o* sound, like *top*. Say the picture words *fox* and *lock*. Do you hear the short-*o* sound?

| top | fox | lock |

Say each picture word. Listen for the short-*o* sound.
Unscramble the letters.

1. l o l d   __ __ l __

2. r f g o   __ r __ __

3. o c s k   __ __ __ k

4. o p s t   __ t __ __

5. l c k c o   __ __ __ c __

Write three other words that have a short-*o* sound.

1. _____

2. _____

3. _____

Name: _____ **Date:** _____

Some words have a short-*u* sound, like *cup*. Say each picture word.
Listen for the short-*u* sound.

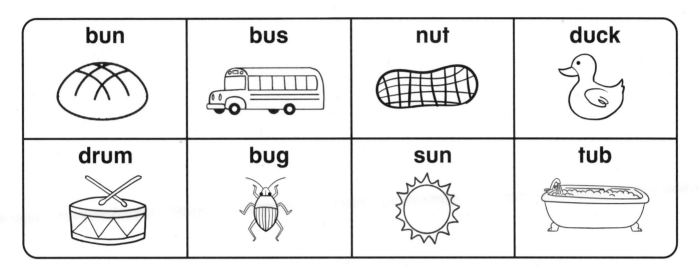

| bun | bus | nut | duck |
| drum | bug | sun | tub |

Find the picture words below. Circle them.
The words may go across or up and down.

t   d   u   c   k   b

u   r   s   u   n   u

b   u   n   r   n   g

v   m   e   b   u   s

j   u   l   p   t   h

Name: _____   Date: _____

Say each picture word below. Listen for the vowel sound.
Then, follow the Color Key.

Color Key				
If the word has the same vowel sound as...				
Color the space...	**blue**	**purple**	**yellow**	**orange**

Use any color for the other spaces.

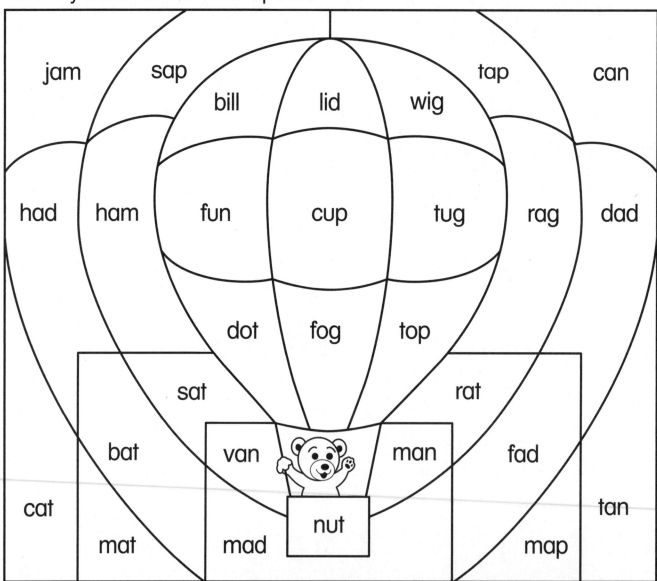

Write the missing letter. Use the Letter Bank. Read the sentence.

I see a h___t-air balloon!

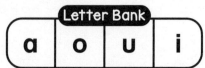

Letter Bank			
a	o	u	i

Name: _____ **Date:** _____

Favorite Animals

Word Bank

| dog | fish | hen | duck | cat |

Read each clue. Write the answer. Use the Word Bank.

1. I rhyme with *pen*.
   But I don't use one.   _____

2. I rhyme with *hat*.
   But I don't wear one.   _____

3. I rhyme with *truck*.
   But I can't drive one.   _____

4. I rhyme with *log*.
   But I don't stay still very long.   _____

5. I rhyme with *dish*.
   But I don't eat on one.   _____

Write About It

Which of the animals above do you like best? Why?

I like the _____ best because

_____

_____

_____

_____

Name: _____ **Date:** _____

Say each picture word. Listen for the beginning sounds of *sc, sk, sm, sn, sp, st,* and *sw*. Circle those letters. Then, connect the dots in the order of the answers. Start at the ♥.

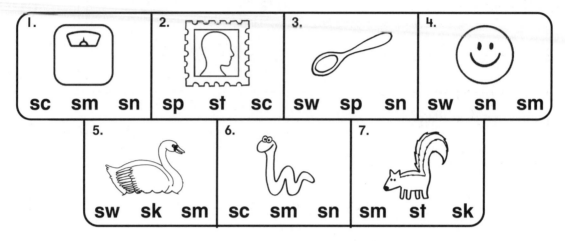

1. sc   sm   sn
2. sp   st   sc
3. sw   sp   sn
4. sw   sn   sm
5. sw   sk   sm
6. sc   sm   sn
7. sm   st   sk

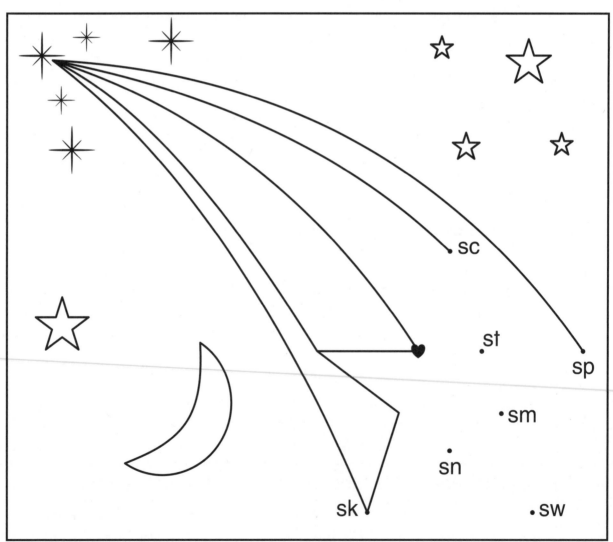

Name: _____ **Date:** _____

Say each picture word in the Color Key.
Listen for the sounds of *bl*, *cl*, *fl*, and *pl*.

Color Key				
If the word has the same beginning sounds as...	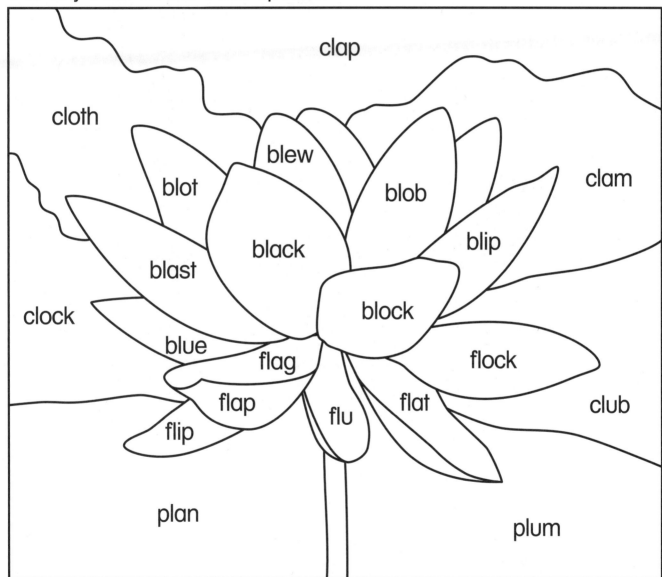			
Color the space...	purple	pink	blue	green

Use any color for the other spaces.

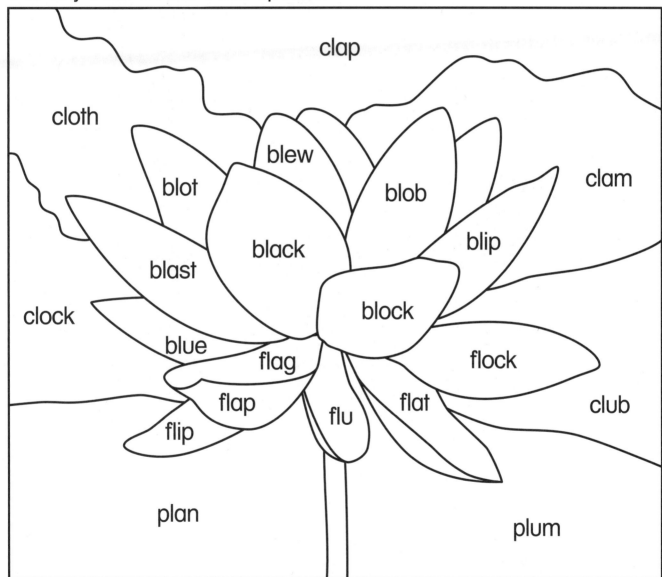

clap

cloth

blew

blot

blob

clam

black

blip

blast

block

clock

blue

flag

flock

flap

flat

club

flip

flu

plan

plum

Write the missing letters. Use the Letter Bank. Read the sentence.

I see a __ __ ower.

Letter Bank			
bl	cl	fl	pl

Name: _____ **Date:** _____

Say each picture word below. Listen for the beginning sounds of *br, cr, dr, fr, gr, pr,* and *tr*. Write the missing letters.

1.  ___ ___ e s s

2. ___ ___ o g

3. ___ ___ e e

4. ___ ___ a p e s

5. ___ ___ a b

6. ___ ___ i c k

7. ___ ___ i z e

Write About It

Write a sentence. Use two of the words above.

_____

Name: _____   **Date:** _____

The letters *scr, spr,* and *str* stand for the beginning sounds you hear in *scrap, spring,* and *street*.

Help Lilly get home. Read the words below. If a word begins with *scr, spr,* and *str,* color the shape red. Then, follow the red shapes.

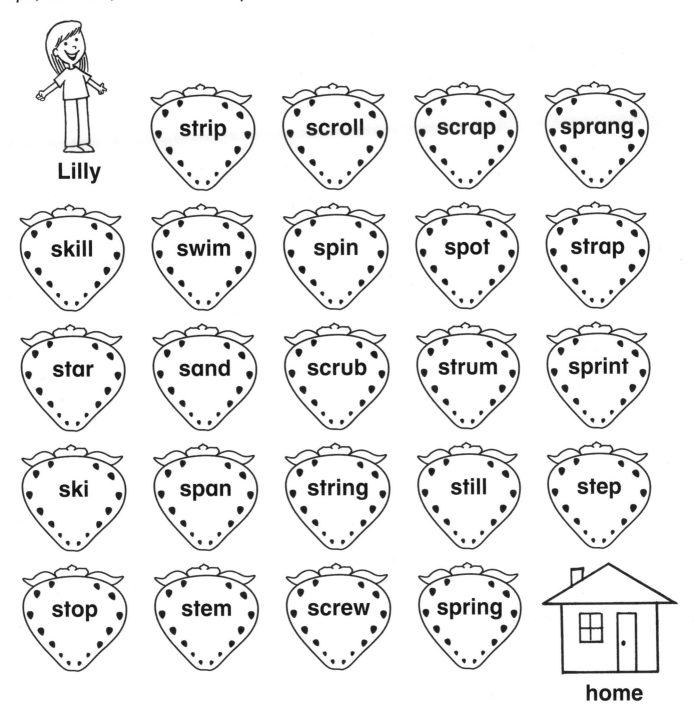

Lilly

strip   scroll   scrap   sprang

skill   swim   spin   spot   strap

star   sand   scrub   strum   sprint

ski   span   string   still   step

stop   stem   screw   spring   home

Name: _____ Date: _____

The letters *spl, squ,* and *thr* stand for the beginning sounds you hear in *splash, square,* and *three.*

Say each picture word. Listen for the sounds of *spl, squ,* and *thr.* Unscramble the letters.

1. [ ] a q s u r e   s __ __ __ __ e

2. l p s a h s   __ __ l __ __ h

3. e t r h e   t __ __ __ __

4. t n h e o r   __ h __ o __ __

5. i l s u q r e r   __ q __ __ r __ __ __

Write two sentences. Use a word from above in each sentence.

1. _____

2. _____

Name: _____ **Date:** _____

The letters _lt_ and _nk_ stand for the ending sounds you hear in _belt_ and _link_. Say each picture word. Listen for the sounds of _lt_ or _nk_. Fill in the missing letters.

be ___ ___	sku ___ ___	sa ___ ___
tru ___ ___	qui ___ ___	ba ___ ___

Find the picture words below. Circle them.
The words may go across or up and down.

```
b  q  u  i  l  t
b  e  l  t  e  r
a  s  a  l  t  u
n  c  r  o  e  n
k  s  k  u  n  k
```

Name: _____   **Date:** _____

The letters *rk* and *mp* stand for the ending sounds you hear in *dark* and *jump*. Say each word in the Word Bank. Listen for the sounds of *rk* and *mp*. Underline the letters.

Word Bank		
park	**fork**	**stamp**
bark	**lamp**	**blimp**

Write the picture word below. Use the Word Bank to help.
Then fill in the puzzle.

Across

2. _____

4. _____

5. _____

Down

1. _____

3. _____

4. _____

Name: _____   **Date:** _____

Write Stuff!

Say each picture word. Listen for the beginning sounds.
Write the missing letters on the lines.

| ___ ___ **ate** | ___ ___ **im** | ___ ___ **ake** | ___ ___ **ow** | ___ ___ **ar** |

Say each picture word. Listen for the ending sounds.
Write the missing letters on the lines.

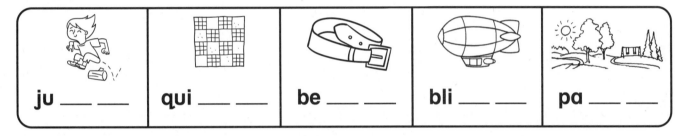

| **ju** ___ ___ | **qui** ___ ___ | **be** ___ ___ | **bli** ___ ___ | **pa** ___ ___ |

Make a poster about your favorite things. Draw pictures of things you
like. Use some of the words above.

Name: _____   **Date:** _____

Two letters can go together to stand for one sound. The letters *s* and *h* stand for the beginning

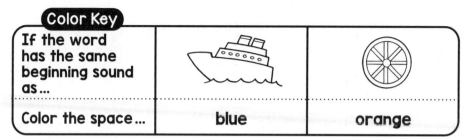

Color Key

If the word has the same beginning sound as...		
Color the space...	**blue**	**orange**

sound in *ship*. The letters *w* and *h* stand for the beginning sound in *wheel*. Follow the Color Key. Use any color for the other spaces.

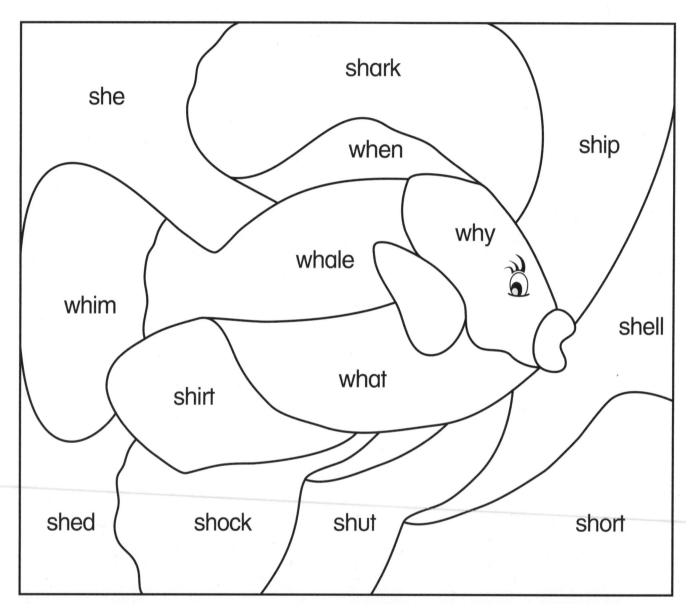

shark

she

when

ship

why

whale

whim

shell

what

shirt

shed   shock   shut   short

Write the missing letters. Use the Letter Bank. Read the sentence.

I see a fi ___ ___ .

Letter Bank

wh	sh	ch	th

Name: _____   Date: _____

Two letters together can stand for one sound. The letters *t* and *h* stand for the beginning sound in *thumb*. They also stand for the ending sound in *path*. The letters *w* and *h* stand for the beginning sound in *whale*.

Say each picture word below. Listen for the sound of *th* or *wh*. Underline those letters.

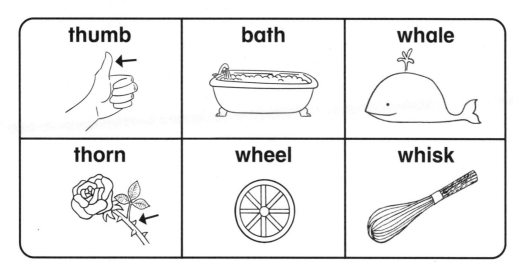

| thumb | bath | whale |
| thorn | wheel | whisk |

Find the picture words below. Circle them.
The words may go across or up and down.

w h e e l w

r u b a t h

t h u m b i

t h o r n s

w h a l e k

Name: _____   **Date:** _____

Two letters can go together to stand for one sound. The letters *c* and *h* stand for the beginning sound in *chain*. They also stand for the ending sound in *patch*. The letters *g* and *h* stand for the ending sound in *cough*.

Help the dog get home. Read the words below. Listen for the sounds of *ch* and *gh*. Color those shapes brown. Then, follow the brown shapes.

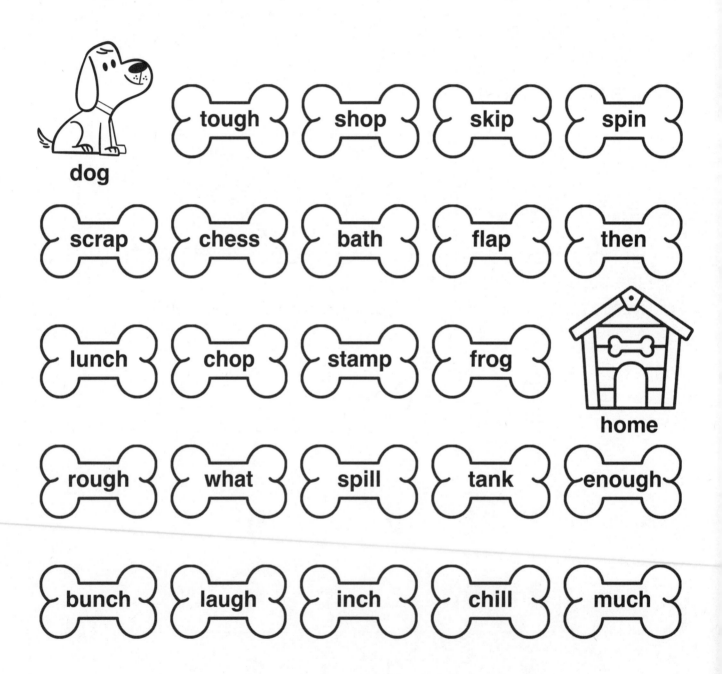

dog

tough   shop   skip   spin

scrap   chess   bath   flap   then

lunch   chop   stamp   frog

home

rough   what   spill   tank   enough

bunch   laugh   inch   chill   much

Name: _____ **Date:** _____

Two letters can go together to stand for one sound. The letters *p* and *h* stand for the beginning sound in *phonics*. The letters *n* and *g* stand for the ending sound in *bring*.

Say each picture word. Listen for the sounds of *ph* and *ng*. Unscramble the letters.

1.   g n i r   r __ __ __

2.   p h t o r y   __ r __ __ __ y

3. ![kite]   t s r i g n   __ __ __ __ __ g

4. ![family photo]   h o p o t   p __ __ __ __

5. ![phone]   e p o h n   __ h __ __ __

Write two sentences. Use a word from above in each sentence.

1. _____

2. _____

Name: _____ Date: _____

Fun With Riddles

Word Bank

| shark | chair | phone | whale |

Read each clue. Write the answer. Use the Word Bank.

1. I have a ring.
   But I don't wear one.   _____

2. I have four legs.
   But I can't walk.   _____

3. I have large teeth.
   But I don't go to the dentist.   _____

4. I am not a teapot.
   But I have a spout.   _____

Write About It

Do you like riddles? Why or why not?

_____

_____

_____

_____

Name: _____   **Date:** _____

Some vowels say the name of the letter. This is called a long-vowel sound. Say the first picture word: *rake*. Do you hear the letter name *a*? Notice that the *e* at the end is silent.

Say the other picture words below. Listen for the long-vowel sounds.

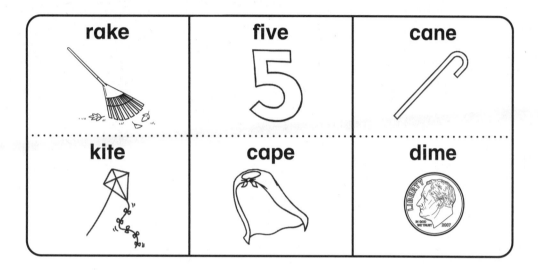

Find the picture words below. Circle them.
The words may go across or up and down.

c a n e l f

r d i m e i

a a o l t v

k c a p e e

e n k i t e

Name: _____   **Date:** _____

A long-vowel sound says the vowel's name. There is a long-*o* sound in the word *cone*. There is a long-*u* sound in the word *cute*. Notice that the letter *e* is silent.

Say each picture word below. Listen for the long-*o* or long-*u* sound. Write the missing letters. Then, write the words in the chart below.

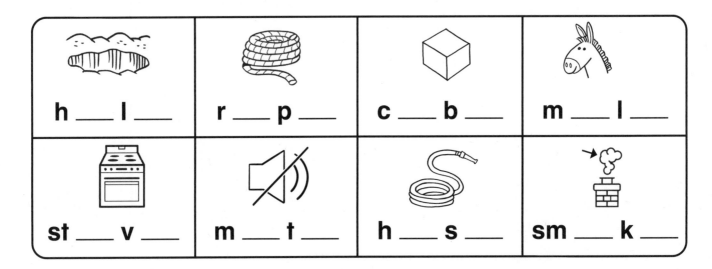

h __ l __	r __ p __	c __ b __	m __ l __
st __ v __	m __ t __	h __ s __	sm __ k __

o_e	u_e

Name: _____   **Date:** _____

Some vowels say the name of the letter. This is called a long-vowel sound. Say the first picture word: *bone.* Do you hear the letter name *o*? Notice that the letter *e* at the end is silent. Say the other picture words below. Listen for the long-vowel sounds.

Start at the bottom and climb to the top. Use the clues.
Then, write the words.

7.   ___ ___ ___ ___

> **Change one letter.**

6.   ___ ___ ___ ___

> **Change one letter.**

5.   ___ ___ ___ ___

> **Change one letter.**

4.   ___ ___ ___ ___

> **Change one letter.**

3.   ___ ___ ___ ___

> **Change one letter.**

2.   ___ ___ ___ ___

> **Change one letter.**

1.   **b   o   n   e**

Name: _____   Date: _____

Summertime Fun!

Word Bank

| bike | skate | kite | note | lake |

Read each clue. Write the answer. Use the Word Bank.

1. I can fly.
   But I am not an airplane.   _____

2. You can put me on your foot.
   But I am not a shoe.   _____

3. You can ride on me.
   But I am not a horse.   _____

4. I have fish.
   But I am not an ocean.   _____

5. I make music.
   But I am not a piano.   _____

Write About It

Write about your favorite things to do in the summer.

_____

_____

_____

Name: _____ **Date:** _____

Some words have a long-*a* sound, like in *rain*. Say each picture word. Listen for the long-*a* sound. Underline the letters that make the long-*a* sound. Then, use the words to fill in the blanks.

clay	steak	sleigh	sail
eight	train	spray	paint

1. Write the words with a long-*a* sound spelled with *ai*.

_____   _____   _____

2. Write the words with a long-*a* sound spelled with *ay*.

_____   _____

3. Write the words with a long-*a* sound spelled with *eigh*.

_____   _____

4. Write the word with a long-*a* sound spelled with *ea*.

_____

Name: _____   Date: _____

Some words have a long-*a* sound, like in *day*. Help Jay get to the birthday party. Say each word below. If the word has a long-*a* sound, color the shape orange. Then, follow the orange shapes.

Jay

clay	rain	tray	break
son	ran	tap	van	stay
pay	gray	weigh	train	neigh
main	gift	cup	box	dish
eight	brain		fan	twig

birthday party

Name: _____   **Date:** _____

Some words have a long-*e* sound, like in *see*. Say each picture word. Listen for the long-*e* sound. Underline the letters that make the long-*e* sound. Then, use the words to fill in the blanks.

me	fifty	key	feet
leaf	field	beach	bee

1. Write the words with a long-*e* sound spelled with *ee*.

_____   _____

2. Write the words with a long-*e* sound spelled with *ea*.

_____   _____

3. Write the word with a long-*e* sound spelled with *e*.

_____

4. Write the word with a long-*e* sound spelled with *ie*.

_____

5. Write the word with a long-*e* sound spelled with *y*.

_____

6. Write the word with a long-*e* sound spelled with *ey*.

_____

Long *e: e, ea, ee, ey, ie, y*

Name: _____ Date: _____

Some words have a long-*e* sound. The letters *ea, ee, ey, ie,* and *y* stand for the long-*e* sound you hear in *beak, tree, key, field,* and *baby.*

beak	tree	key	field	baby

Say each picture word. Listen for the long-*e* sound.
Unscramble the letters.

1. p e l s e   s __ __ __ __

2. e p a h c   __ __ a __ __

3. f h t e i   __ __ i e __

4. y p n e n   p __ __ __ __

5. y e t k u r   __ u __ __ __ __

Write two sentences. Use a word from above in each sentence.

1. _____

2. _____

Name: _____ Date: _____

Some words have a long-*i* sound, like in *my*. Say each picture word. Listen for the long-*i* sound. Underline the letters that stand for the long-*i* sound. Then, use the words to fill in the blanks.

child	pie	knight	fly
climb	thigh	sky	tie

1. Write the words with a long-*i* sound spelled with an *i*.

_____   _____

2. Write the words with a long-*i* sound spelled with a *y*.

_____   _____

3. Write the words with a long-*i* sound spelled with *ie*.

_____   _____

4. Write the words with a long-*i* sound spelled with *igh*.

_____   _____

Name: _____ **Date:** _____

Some words have a long-*i* sound. The long-*i* sound may be spelled with an *i* (as in *kind*), *ie* (as in *tie*), *igh* (as in *high*), or *y* (as in *my*).

Say each picture word below. Listen for the long-*i* sound.
Write the missing letters.

1.   c r ___

2.   l ___ ___ ___ t

3.   p ___ ___

4.   f l ___

5.   n ___ ___ ___ t

6.    c l ___ m b

7.   t h ___ ___ ___

8.   s l ___ d ___

Name: _____   **Date:** _____

Some words have a long-*o* sound, like in *hold*. Say each picture word. Listen for the long-*o* sound. Underline the letters that stand for the long-*o* sound. Then, use the words to fill in the blanks.

coal	toe	snow	hoe
gold	boat	cold	crow

1. Write the words with a long-*o* sound spelled with *o*.

_____   _____

2. Write the words with a long-*o* sound spelled with *oa*.

_____   _____

3. Write the words with a long-*o* sound spelled with *ow*.

_____   _____

4. Write the words with a long-*o* sound spelled with *oe*.

_____   _____

Name: _____   Date: _____

Some words have a long-*o* sound, like in *row*. Say each picture word.
Listen for the long-*o* sound.

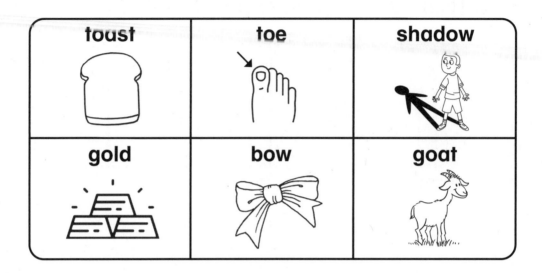

Find the picture words below. Circle them.
The words may go across or up and down.

g o l d t f

o r i m o g

a s t l e b

t o a s t o

s h a d o w

Name: _____ **Date:** _____

Some words have a long-*u* sound, like in *few*. Say each picture word. Listen for the long-*u* sound. Underline the letters that stand for the long-*u* sound. Then, use the words to fill in the blanks.

1. Write the words with a long-*u* sound spelled with *u*.

_____ _____

_____ _____

2. Write the words with a long-*u* sound spelled with *ue*.

_____ _____

3. Write the word with a long-*u* sound spelled with *ew*.

_____

Name: _____   **Date:** _____

Some words have a long-*u* sound, like in *Utah*. Help the pupil get to the museum. Say each word in the puzzle. If the word has a long-*u* sound, color the shape red. Then, follow the red shapes.

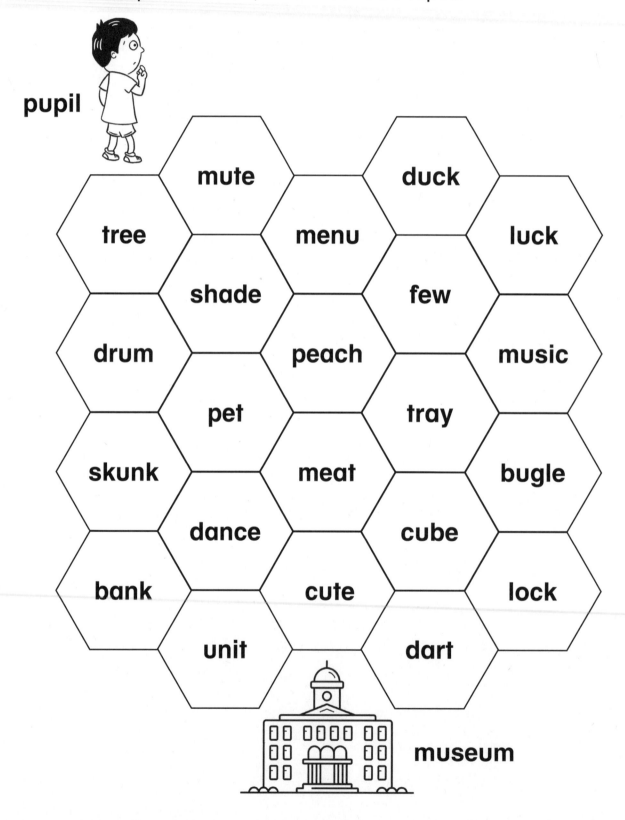

pupil

mute · duck · tree · menu · luck · shade · few · drum · peach · music · pet · tray · skunk · meat · bugle · dance · cube · bank · cute · lock · unit · dart

museum

Name: _____   Date: _____

Food Favorites

Word Bank

| pie | steak | toast | menu | peas |

Read each clue. Write the answer. Use the Word Bank.

1. I have a long-*e* sound.
I am a vegetable.   _____

2. I have a long-*i* sound.
I can have fruits inside.   _____

3. I have a long-*o* sound.
I am made from bread.   _____

4. I have a long-*a* sound.
I am a kind of meat.   _____

5. I have a long-*u* sound.
I show a list of food.   _____

Write About It

What are your favorite foods?

_____

_____

_____

_____

Name: _____   **Date:** _____

Sometimes the letters *oo* can stand for a long sound, like in *moon* and *food*.

Say each picture word. Listen for the long-*oo* sound. Unscramble the letters.

1.  o h c s o l   s __ __ __ __ __

2.  o s o g e   __ __ o __ __

3.  p o s n o   __ __ __ __ n

4.  o m o b r   b __ __ __ __

5.  o p o l   __ o __ __

Write two sentences. Use a word from above in each sentence.

1. _____

2. _____

Name: _____   **Date:** _____

Sometimes the letters *oo* can stand for a short sound, like in *foot* and *took*. Say each picture word. Listen for the short-*oo* sound.

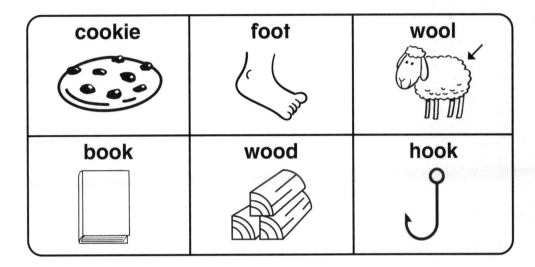

| cookie | foot | wool |
| book | wood | hook |

Find the words above and circle them.
The words may go across or up and down.

c   o   o   k   i   e

f   w   o   o   l   b

o   o   p   l   e   o

o   o   t   o   w   o

t   d   h   o   o   k

Name: _____   **Date:** _____

The letters *oi* and *oy* stand for the sound you hear in the middle of *boil* and *joy*. Say each word in the Word Bank. Listen for the sound of *oi* and *oy*. Underline the letters.

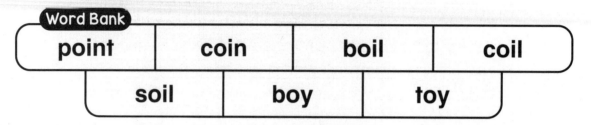

Word Bank

point	coin	boil	coil

soil	boy	toy

Write the picture word below. Use the Word Bank to help.
Then fill in the puzzle.

Across

4. _____

5. _____

6. _____

Down

1. _____

2. _____

3. _____

4. _____

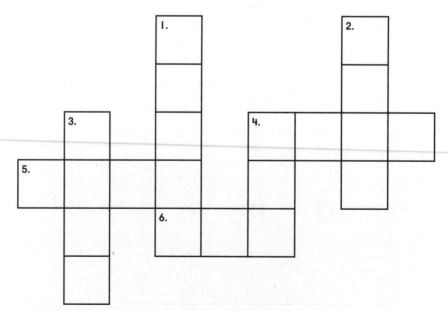

Name: _____ Date: _____

The letters *ou* and *ow* stand for the sound you hear in the middle of *house* and *crown*. Follow the Color Key. Use any color for the other spaces.

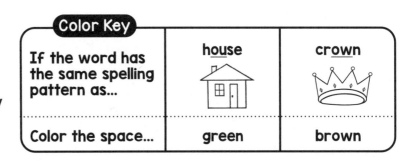

Color Key		
If the word has the same spelling pattern as...	house 🏠	crown 👑
Color the space...	green	brown

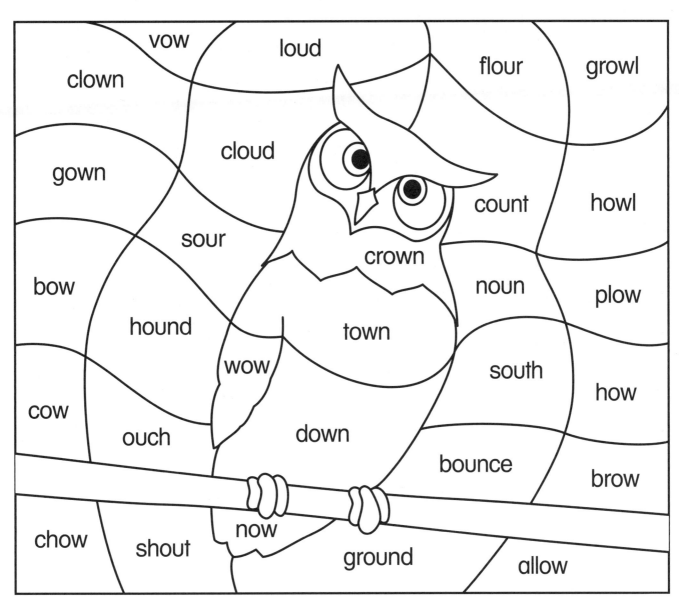

vow loud flour growl clown cloud gown sour count howl crown bow hound town noun plow wow cow ouch down south how chow shout now ground bounce brow allow

Write the missing letters. Use the Letter Bank. Read the sentence.

I see an ___ ___ l.

Letter Bank	
ow	ou

Name: _____ **Date:** _____

The letters *er*, *ir*, and *ur* stand for the same sounds you hear in the middle of *verb*, *sir*, and *turn*.

Say each picture word. Write the missing letters.
Then, write the words in the chart below.

 g ___ ___ l	 sh ___ ___ t	 t ___ ___ tle	 h ___ ___ d
 n ___ ___ se	 b ___ ___ d	 d ___ ___ t	 dinn ___ ___

er	ir	ur

Name: _____ **Date:** _____

The letters *oar, or,* and *ore* stand for the same sounds you hear in the middle of *board, horn*, and *core*. Look at the spelling patterns below. Then, follow the Color Key to help each bee get to the hive.

Color Key			
If the word has this spelling pattern...	*oar*	*or*	*ore*
Color the space...	blue	purple	yellow

boar · oar · board · soar

burn · fur · girl · yard · roar

bird · corn · fork · hive

dorm · torn · fort · snore · chore

core · wore · sore · star

Name: _____ Date: _____

The letters *ar* stand for the sounds you hear at the beginning of *arm*.
Say the picture words *yarn* and *star*. Do you hear the same sounds?

arm	yarn	star

Say each picture word. Listen for the sounds of *ar*.
Unscramble the letters.

1. h a s r k   __ __ __ r __

2. a b r n   __ __ __ n

3. a c d r   __ __ r __

4. t h c r a   __ h __ __ __

5. p h r a   __ __ __ p

Write two other words that have the same ending sounds as in *car*.

1. _____

2. _____

Name: _____ Date: _____

The letters *air* stand for the same sounds you hear at the end of *chair*. The letters *are* and *ear* stand for the same sounds you hear at the end of *rare* and *pear*.

Say each picture word. Write the missing letters. Then, write the words in the chart below.

ch __ __ __   squ __ __ __   b __ __ __   st __ __ __

p __ __ __   h __ __ __   m __ __ __

air	are	ear

Name: _____ **Date:** _____

Farm Life

Word Bank

| goose | horse | farm | cow | corn |

Read each clue. Write the answer. Use the Word Bank.

1. I can fly.
But I don't usually land at airports. _____

2. I have ears.
But I can't hear. _____

3. I have a mane.
But I am not a zebra. _____

4. I have the little word *arm*.
But I don't have a hand. _____

5. I can give you milk.
But I don't have cookies. _____

Write About It

Write about your favorite things to do on a farm.

_____

_____

_____

_____

Name: _____ Date: _____

Plural means "more than one." The picture words *dogs* and *gifts* show more than one. We can add *s* at the end of a word to make it plural.

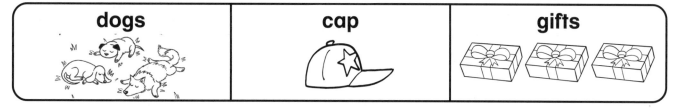

dogs	cap	gifts

Say each picture word. Unscramble the letters.

1.   t s a n   ___ ___ ___ ___

2.    l a b l   ___ ___ ___ ___

3.    b s o t o   ___ ___ ___ ___ ___

4.   a s h t   ___ ___ ___ ___

5.   r f o k   ___ ___ ___ ___

Write a plural word. _____

Draw a picture.

Name: _____ **Date:** _____

Singular means "one." *Plural* means "more than one."

Color Key		
If the word is...	**singular**	**plural**
Color the space...	pink	black

Use any color for the other spaces.

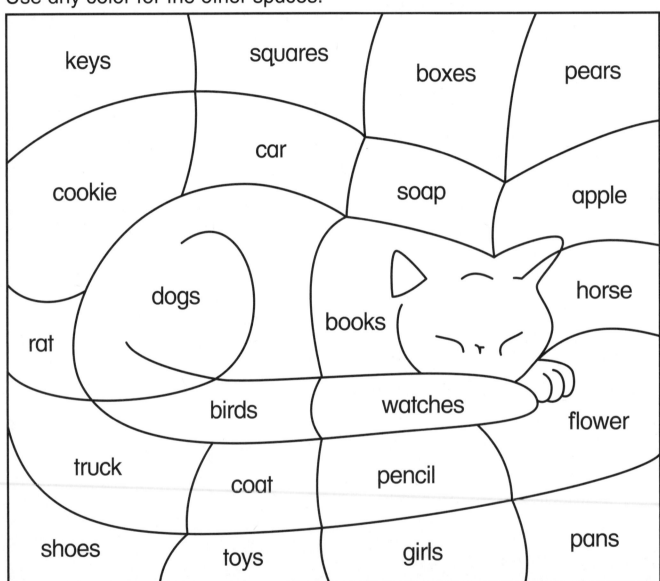

keys   squares   boxes   pears

car

cookie   soap   apple

dogs   horse

rat   books

birds   watches   flower

truck   coat   pencil

shoes   toys   girls   pans

Write the missing word. Use the Word Bank. Read the sentence.

I see a _____.

Word Bank

| cat | cats |

Name: _____ **Date:** _____

Say each picture word. Count the syllables.
Then, use the words to fill in the blanks.

bat	baseball	game	bicycle
rocket	doll	robot	basketball

1. Write the words with one syllable.

_____   _____   _____

2. Write the words with two syllables.

_____   _____   _____

3. Write the words with three syllables.

_____   _____

4. Write the name of your favorite toy.

How many syllables does the word have? Circle. 1 2 3 4

Name: _____   **Date:** _____

Say each picture word. Count the syllables. Color the pictures with one syllable gray. Color the pictures with two syllables red. Color the picture with three syllables orange.

Find the picture words below. Circle them.
The words may go across or up and down.

a   c   e   t   y   m   n

p   r   a   b   b   i   t

p   c   s   a   p   r   e

l   a   n   t   e   r   n

e   t   o   m   a   t   o

Name: _____   **Date:** _____

A prefix comes at the beginning of a word and changes its meaning.

Word Bank		
re- (again)	**pre-** (before)	**un-** (not or opposite of)
remake = make again	**pre**test = test before	**un**happy = not happy

Read each definition. Unscramble the letters.

1. cook before   c e k o p o r   __ r __ __ __ __ k

2. do again   d r e o   __ __ __ o

3. opposite of *tie*   t u i n e   __ __ t __ __

4. not well   l n w u e l   __ n __ __ __ l

5. build again   b u r e i d l   __ __ __ u __ __ __

What does the word *resend* mean?
Use what you know about the prefix *re-* to help.

_____

_____

_____

_____

Name: _____ **Date:** _____

A prefix comes at the beginning of a word and changes its meaning. Read each definition. Write the word. Use the Prefix Bank to help.

Prefix Bank		
re- (again)	**pre-** (before)	**un-** (not or opposite of)

use again _____

plan before _____

to cook before _____

not kind _____

fill again _____

not paid _____

Find the words you wrote. Circle them.
The words may go across or up and down.

p	r	e	c	o	o	k
r	e	u	s	e	w	u
e	f	e	g	a	r	n
p	i	l	u	e	i	k
l	l	w	v	n	n	i
a	l	t	i	x	d	n
n	u	n	p	a	i	d

Name: _____ Date: _____

A suffix comes at the end of a word and changes its meaning.
Read each definition. Write the word. Use the Suffix Bank to help.

Suffix Bank		
-ful (full of)	**-less** (without)	**-able** (able to be)

full of joy   _____   full of cheer   _____

without harm _____   without spots   _____

able to wash _____   full of care   _____

Find the words you wrote. Circle them.
The words may go across or up and down.

```
h   a   r   m   l   e   s   s
a   h   c   p   e   r   j   c
k   r   t   e   c   a   o   h
w   a   s   h   a   b   l   e
t   m   v   e   r   z   y   e
z   e   r   k   e   m   v   r
i   j   o   y   f   u   l   f
w   s   c   l   u   s   i   u
x   q   r   p   l   a   b   l
s   p   o   t   l   e   s   s
```

Name: _____   Date: _____

A suffix comes at the end of a word and changes its meaning. Say each word in the Word Bank. Underline the suffix.

Word Bank		
playful	**wearable**	**hopeless**
breakable	**useful**	**washable**

Read the definition. Write the word that goes with it. Use the Word Bank to help. Then, fill in the puzzle.

Across	**Down**
1. without hope _____	2. full of play _____
3. able to wear _____	3. able to wash _____
5. full of use _____	4. able to break _____

Name: _____   **Date:** _____

Sometimes two words can be put together. The new word is called a *compound word*. The words *cook* and *book* can be put together to make *cookbook*.

Look at the picture words that make up the compound word. Unscramble the letters.

1. | o l t a f b l o

___ ___ ___ t ___ ___ ___ l

2. | n f u l w s r e o

___ ___ ___ f ___ ___ w ___ ___

3. | i b x m o a l

___ ___ ___ l ___ ___ x

4. | l r o b d e o l

___ ___ ___ r ___ ___ ___ l

5. | h r s s o o e e h

___ ___ r ___ ___ ___ o ___

Name: _____ **Date:** _____

Make compound words. Match the words on the left
to the words on the right.

1.	rain	hopper
2.	bird	brush
3.	rail	fish
4.	grass	road
5.	tooth	house
6.	note	shelf
7.	gold	coat
8.	book	book

Think of a compound word. Keep it secret. Draw a picture that shows
each part of the word. Show a friend your pictures. Can they guess the
compound word?

Name: _____   Date: _____

Ocean Favorites

Word Bank

sail	star	sea	gull

shell	boat	fish

Read each clue. Put the words together to make a compound word. Use the Word Bank. You can use each word more than once.

1. I am a boat.
The wind makes me move.   _____

2. I am a fish.
But I look like a star.   _____

3. I am a bird.
I live near the water.   _____

4. I am a shell.
I come from the sea.   _____

Write About It

What are your favorite things about the ocean?

_____

_____

_____

_____

Phonics and Word-Study Games

Beat the Clock

This hidden letter game pairs fun with learning as children identify beginning, middle, and ending letters in picture words.

You will need:

- Picture Cards (pages 76–77) • scissors
- small sticky notes • two tables

Before you begin:

Make two copies of the Picture Cards on cardstock and cut apart each set of cards. Using small sticky notes, cover one of the letters in each picture word. Make sure some beginning, middle, and ending letters are covered. Place each set of Picture Cards on a table and spread the cards face up.

To play:

Form two teams of three or four players each and assign each team a table. When you say *go*, players have two minutes to look at each Picture Card on the table, identify the missing letter, and write it on the sticky note. The team that correctly identifies the most hidden letters wins.

Hop or Drop?

This silly game is sure to amuse children while reinforcing their understanding of the soft and hard sounds of the letters g and c.

Before you begin:

Remind children that the letter *g* has two sounds: a hard sound (like in *gate*) and a soft sound (like in *giraffe*).

To play:

Have children stand in an open area. Tell them you will call out different words. If you say a word with a soft-*g* sound, they should hop one time. If you say a word that has a hard-*g* sound, they should sit on the ground. Tell children to listen carefully because the *g* sound can come in the beginning, middle, or end of the word. Use the words below to get started. Let the fun begin!

Words with a hard-*g* sound

go, gum, gate, guitar, goat, goose, ghost, girl, golf, tiger, eagle, seagull, bug, dog, big, fog, rug

Words with a soft-*g* sound

giraffe, gel, gym, germs, gem, giant, ginger, gentle, angel, danger, age, orange, engine

Variation:

Follow the same procedure, but this time play the game using hard- and soft-*c* sounds.

Words with a hard-*c* sound

clay, camp, cook, corn, cake, clock, carrot, come, cry, car, crisp, cup, bacon, because, scare

Words with a soft-*c* sound

cycle, cell, celery, centipede, center, circle, cereal, cement, decide, pencil, fancy, recipe, circus

Picture Card Art

In this game, children sharpen their artistic skills while reinforcing their knowledge of short-vowel sounds.

You will need:

- Picture Cards (pages 76–77) • scissors
- small paper bag • whiteboard (or chart paper) • dry-erase marker

Before you begin:

Photocopy the Picture Cards onto cardstock. Cut apart the cards and place them in a paper bag.

Review short-vowel sounds using simple words with the consonant-vowel-consonant (CVC) pattern, such as *bat, ten, dig, fox,* and *bus.* Show children some of the Picture Cards and have them identify the short-vowel sounds in each word.

To play:

Divide players into two teams. Every player on each team takes a turn at being the artist. At each team's turn, the artist takes a Picture Card from the paper bag and begins drawing a picture of the object on the board (or chart paper). The other players (on both teams) try to guess the object. To score a point for their team, players must correctly identify the object, spell the word, and identify the short-vowel sound. Next, a player from the other team becomes the artist. Play continues until every player on each team has taken a turn as the artist. The team with the most points wins.

Wild Card Concentration

In this two-player version of the classic game Concentration, children identify rhyming words.

You will need:

- Picture Cards (pages 76–77) • scissors

Before you begin:

Photocopy the Picture Cards onto cardstock. Cut apart the cards. Lay out the cards face down on a table.

To play:

Players take turns choosing two cards and turning them over. If the words on the Picture Cards rhyme, the player keeps both cards and takes another turn. If the words do not rhyme, the player turns the cards back over. When all the cards have been taken, the player with the most Picture Cards wins.

Phonics Tic-Tac-Toe

This small-group game challenges players to substitute vowel sounds to make new words.

You will need:

- Picture Cards (pages 76–77) • scissors
- small paper bag • whiteboard • dry-erase marker

Before you begin:

Photocopy the Picture Cards onto cardstock. Cut apart the cards. Place the following Picture Cards in a paper bag: *pan, cat, net, mat, dig, wig, fin, win, top, mop, cot, sun, run, bug, rug.* Draw a large tic-tac-toe grid on the board.

To play:

Divide the players into two teams. Designate each team as X or O. Have players from each team take turns taking a Picture Card out of the paper bag. The player says the word on the Picture Card. If the player can change the vowel sound to make a new word, the player may write their symbol (X or O) on the tic-tac-toe grid. For instance, a player draws the word *cat* and changes the *a* to an *o* to make the new word *cot*. The first team to have three marks in a row wins.

Variation:

Play the game again, but this time have players change the beginning sound to make a new word. For instance, a player draws the word *sun* and changes the *s* to an *f* and make the new word *fun*. Use all Picture Cards for this version of the game.

Go Fish With Rhymes

Reinforce rhyming skills with this two-player variation of the classic game Go Fish.

You will need:

- Picture Cards (pages 76–77) • scissors

Before you begin:

Photocopy the Picture Cards onto cardstock. Cut apart the cards.

To play:

Shuffle the Pictures Cards and deal each player five cards. Stack the rest of the cards face down between the players. Players look at their cards to see whether any of them have rhyming words. If they do, they place their rhyming cards in front of them face up on the table. If they don't have rhyming cards, players take turns asking each other for a card that rhymes with a card in their hand. For instance, a player might say, "Do you have a card that rhymes with *can*?" If the other player has a rhyming card, they must give it to the asking player. If not, they tell the asking player to "Go fish." The asking player then takes a card from the stack. If the asking player gets a card that rhymes with their card, they should place both cards face up on the table. The game ends when one player is out of cards or there are no cards left in the stack. The player with the most matches wins.

Musical Rhymes

Combine music and rhyming words for a fun-filled activity that is sure to amuse!

You will need:

- Picture Cards (pages 76–77) • scissors
- music

Before you begin:

Photocopy the Picture Cards onto cardstock. Cut apart the cards. Notice there are 24 Picture Cards, and each card is part of a rhyming pair (for instance, *can* and *pan*).

To play:

Pass out a Picture Card to each player. Tell the children that when you start the music, they should walk around the room looking for a player whose card has a word that rhymes with theirs and then sit down together before the music stops. When the music stops, the players with rhyming cards share the words on their cards with the class. If there are players who did not find a match in the first round, start the music again until everyone has found a match. Invite those players to share the words on their cards with the class.

Build-a-Word

In this word-building game, team members work together to create words with consonant blends.

You will need:

- letter tiles • index cards • marker

Before you begin:

Write each of the following *r*-blends on an index card: *br, cr, dr, fr, gr, pr,* and *tr.* Spread them on a table face up.

Before playing the game, review *r*-blends. Write the words *break, crane,* and *drill* on the board. Underline the *r*-blends and point out that when *br, cr,* and *dr* go together in a word, the sounds of both letters are often blended together. Then, say each word and emphasize the blended sound of the first two letters. Tell children that there are other *r*-blends, such as *fr, gr, pr,* and *tr.* As a group, generate words for each *r*-blend, such as *frog, green, price,* and *train.*

To play:

Divide the class into groups of two or three players each. Give each group several sets of letter tiles from *a* to *z*. Call on a volunteer from each team to select an *r*-blend index card. Then, have the group work together to build several words that start with the *r*-blend. Afterward, invite each group to share their words with the class.

For even more fun, set a timer for three minutes and have groups compete to see who can build the most words. (Note: If each team has only two sets of letter tiles, there may not be enough letters to create three or more words with the same beginning blend. Have children write the *r*-blend for each word on an index card and use letter tiles to complete the word.)

Variation:

Follow the same procedure, but this time use *l*-blends. Before you begin, write one of the following *l*-blends on an index card: *bl, cl, fl, gl, pl,* and *sl.*

Word Sort Relay

This challenging game calls for fast thinking and is a great way to review consonant digraphs.

You will need:

- index cards • marker • two buckets or cans

Before you begin:

Write each of the following *ch* and *wh* words on an index card: *chat, chick, chin, chart, chip, chop, chow, chap, chunk, chill, child, chief, chalk, watch, patch, what, whip, why, white, whirl, wheel, whale, whine, whistle, when, what, wheat, where.*

Review consonant digraphs. Remind children that when some letters go together, they make a new sound. For instance, the letters *c* and *h* go together to make the beginning sound in *chair.* Point out that the *ch* can also appear at the end of a word, like in *catch.* Explain that the letters *w* and *h* go together and make the beginning sound in *whale* and *whistle.*

To play:

To prepare for the game, divide the class into two teams. Have the teams stand in single-file lines beside each other. Place the buckets about five yards away from the teams. Place a stack of the index cards you made beside each bucket. On one bucket write the letters *ch*, and on the other bucket write the letters *wh*.

When you say *go*, hand the first two players index cards and tell them to run as fast as they can to the buckets, read the word on the index card, and deposit it in the bucket that has the matching consonant digraph. Next, they should pick up an index card from the stack beside the bucket, run back, and hand it to the next player in the line. Then, the next player repeats the same process. The first team to successfully deposit all their index cards in the correct bucket wins.

Hula-Hoop Hop

In this small-group activity, children strengthen their understanding of long-vowel sounds while enjoying hula-hoop hopping fun!

You will need:

• two or three hula-hoops

Before you begin:

Review the long-a sound. Remind players that the most common spellings for the long-a sound are a_e (*bake*), ai (*mail*), and ay (*hay*). As a group, generate a list of words with each spelling.

To play:

Place hula-hoops end to end in an open space. Have players form a line behind the hula-hoops. The first player says a word with a long-a sound. If correct, the player hops into the first hoop. Next, the same player says another word with a long-a sound. If it is correct, the player may hop into the next hoop, and so on. (If players cannot think of a word with a long-a sound, they can ask teammates for help.) The next player then takes a turn.

After all the players have hopped through all the hoops, start again but choose a different vowel sound this time.

Two (or Three) Words in One!

Five-minute games are a great way to maximize your time while waiting for lunch or special activities. This game enhances children's listening and thinking skills.

To play:

Tell children that in some words, you can rearrange the letters to make new words. For instance, the letters in *tab* can be rearranged to spell *bat*. Say one of the words below. Challenge children to rearrange the letters to make a new word.

rat – *tar, art*	**top** – *pot, opt*
won – *now, own*	**nap** – *pan*
ton – *not*	**pal** – *lap*
ape – *pea*	**pit** – *tip*
meal – *male, lame*	**star** – *rats, arts*
palm – *lamp*	**post** – *tops, stop*

Syllable Scavenger Hunt

Help advanced learners reinforce their knowledge of syllabication with this searching game.

You will need:

• paper (for each pair of children) • pencils

Before you begin:

Review syllabication. Remind children that a syllable is a unit of pronunciation that has one vowel sound. Provide children with examples of one-, two-, and three-syllable words.

To play:

Pair up children. When you say *go*, have children go on a classroom scavenger hunt and look for words that have one, two, and three syllables. Have them record the words on a sheet of paper. After everyone has completed the scavenger hunt, ask each pair to share the words they found one at a time while the other children identify the number of syllables in each word.

Wordsmith Fun!

This fast-paced game challenges players to combine prefixes and root words to create the most words possible in three minutes.

Before you begin:

Review how to build words with prefixes. Then, write the following prefixes and root words on the board: *re-, pre-, un-, work, play, happy, test, print, do, tie, wrap, heat.*

To play:

When you say *go*, players have three minutes to write as many words as possible using the prefixes and root words on the board. They may use each prefix and root word multiple times. The player who writes the most words wins.

Variation:

Challenge children to build as many words as possible in three minutes using the following suffixes and root words: *-ful, -less, -able, cheer, help, fear, drink, break, hope, care, read, spot.*

Time for Charades!

This all-time favorite guessing game is a great way to reinforce children's understanding of compound words.

Before you begin:

Remind children that compound words are two words put together to make a new word. For instance, the words *book* and *end* can be combined to make the new word *bookend*.

To play:

Write the following words on the board: *see, rail, ball, book, side, flower, sea, bell, box, sun, rain, saw, horse, door, drop, mail, road, cook, foot, walk.* Challenge children to use the words to write three or four compound words on a sheet of paper at their desks. Tell them to keep the words hidden.

Next, invite a volunteer to choose one of their compound words and act out each part of the compound word without using words. Challenge the other children to identify the compound word. The person who guesses the word correctly will take a turn acting out one of their compound words.

Picture Cards

c a n

p a n

c a t

m a t

n e t

w e t

h e n

p e n

d i g

b u g

r u g

c a p

w i g

l i p

z i p

t o p

m o p

d o t

c o t

s u n

r u n

m a p

w i n

f i n

Answer Key

Page 7
I see a big turtle.

Page 8
1. d 2. t 3. n 4. g 5. l 6. b 7. r
8. k 9. p 10. f 11. m 12. s

Page 9
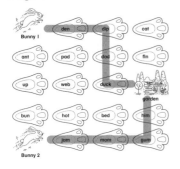

Page 10
1. wrist 2. lamb 3. comb 4. write
5. thumb

Page 11
dog, rain, hat, coat, pants, boots

Page 12

b	d	v	c	a	n
c	a	p	o	l	c
j	n	w	r	c	i
v	c	r	n	e	t
c	e	n	t	r	y

Page 13

Soft *g*	Hard *g*
gem	leg
cage	gift
giraffe	gate
	log
	guitar

Page 14
1. goat 2. goose 3. pigeon
4. giraffe

Page 15
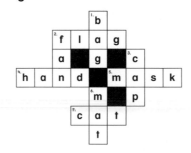

Page 16
1. ten 2. hen 3. men 4. pen
5. pet 6. net

Page 17

Page 18
1. doll 2. frog 3. sock 4. stop
5. clock

Page 19

t	d	u	c	k	b
u	r	s	u	n	u
b	u	n	r	n	g
v	m	e	b	u	s
j	u	l	p	t	h

Page 20
I see a hot-air balloon.

Page 21
1. hen 2. cat 3. duck 4. dog
5. fish

Page 22
1. sc 2. st 3. sp 4. sm 5. sw
6. sn 7. sk

Page 23
I see a flower.

Page 24
1. dress 2. frog 3. tree 4. grapes
5. crab 6. brick 7. prize

Page 25
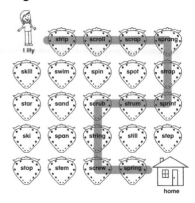

Page 26
1. square 2. splash 3. three
4. throne 5. squirrel

Page 27
belt, skunk, salt, trunk, quilt, bank

b	q	u	i	l	t
b	e	l	t	e	r
a	s	a	l	t	u
n	c	r	o	e	n
k	s	k	u	n	k

Page 28
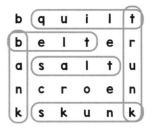

Page 29
skate, swim, snake, snow, star
jump, quilt, belt, blimp, park

Page 30
I see a fish.

Page 31

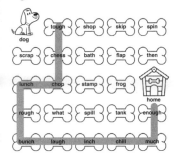

Page 32

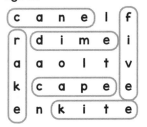

Page 33
1. ring 2. trophy 3. string 4. photo
5. phone

Page 34
1. phone 2. chair 3. shark 4. whale

Page 35

c a n e l f
r d i m e i
a a o l t v
k c a p e e
e n k i t e

Page 36

o_e	u_e
hole	cube
rope	mule
stove	mute
hose	
smoke	

Page 37
1. bone 2. cone 3. cane 4. cake
5. bake 6. bike 7. hike

Page 38
1. kite 2. skate 3. bike 4. lake
5. note

Page 39
1. sail, train, paint 2. clay, spray
3. sleigh, eight 4. steak

Page 40

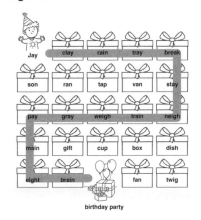

Page 41
1. feet, bee 2. leaf, beach 3. me
4. field 5. fifty 6. key

Page 42
1. sleep 2. peach 3. thief 4. penny
5. turkey

Page 43
1. child, climb 2. fly, sky 3. pie, tie
4. knight, thigh

Page 44
1. cry 2. light 3. pie 4. fly
5. night 6. climb 7. thigh 8. slide

Page 45
1. gold, cold 2. coal, boat 3. snow, crow 4. toe, hoe

Page 46

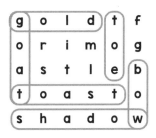

Page 47
1. uniform, music, menu, bugle
2. fuel, rescue 3. pew

Page 48

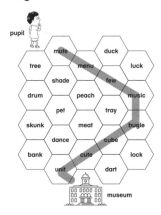

Page 49
1. peas 2. pie 3. toast 4. steak
5. menu

Page 50
1. school 2. goose 3. spoon
4. broom 5. pool

Page 51

Page 52

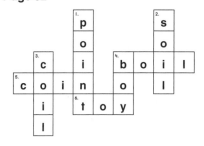

Page 53
I see an owl.

Page 54

ir	er	ur
girl	herd	turtle
shirt	dinner	nurse
bird		
dirt		

Page 55

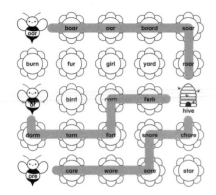

Page 56
1. shark   2. barn   3. card   4. chart   5. harp

Page 57

air	*are*	*ear*
chair	square	bear
stair	mare	pear
hair		

Page 58
1. goose   2. corn   3. horse   4. farm   5. cow

Page 59
1. ants   2. ball   3. boots   4. hats   5. fork

Page 60
I see a cat.

Page 61
1. bat, game, doll   2. baseball, rocket, robot
3. bicycle, basketball   4. Answers will vary.

Page 62

```
a  c  e  t  y  m  n
p  r  a  b  b  i  t
p  c  s  a  p  r  e
l  a  n  t  e  r  n
e  t  o  m  a  t  o
```

Page 63
1. precook   2. redo   3. untie   4. unwell   5. rebuild

Page 64

```
p  r  e  c  o  o  k
r  e  u  s  e  w  u
e  f  e  g  a  r  n
p  i  l  u  e  i  k
l  l  w  v  n  n  i
a  t  t  i  x  d  n
n  u  n  p  a  i  d
```

Page 65

```
h  a  r  m  l  e  s  s
a  h  c  p  e  r  j  c
k  r  t  e  c  a  o  h
w  a  s  h  a  b  l  e
t  m  v  e  r  z  y  e
z  e  r  k  e  m  v  r
i  j  o  y  f  u  l  f
w  s  c  l  u  s  i  u
x  q  r  p  l  a  b  l
s  p  o  t  l  e  s  s
```

Page 66

```
¹h  o  ²p  e  l  e  s  s
        l
    ³w  e  a  r  a  ⁴b  l  e
        a     y           r
        s     f           e
        h     u           a
        a     l           k
        b                 a
⁵u  s  e  f  u  l          b
        e                 l
                          e
```

Page 67
1. football   2. sunflower   3. mailbox   4. doorbell
5. horseshoe

Page 68
1. raincoat   2. birdhouse   3. railroad   4. grasshopper
5. toothbrush   6. notebook   7. goldfish   8. bookshelf

Page 69
1. sailboat   2. starfish   3. seagull   4. seashell